The Official
Manchester City
Annual 2008

Written by David Clayton

A Grange Publication

Photographs © Empics & MCFC
ISBN 978-1-905426-87-4

£6.99

Contents

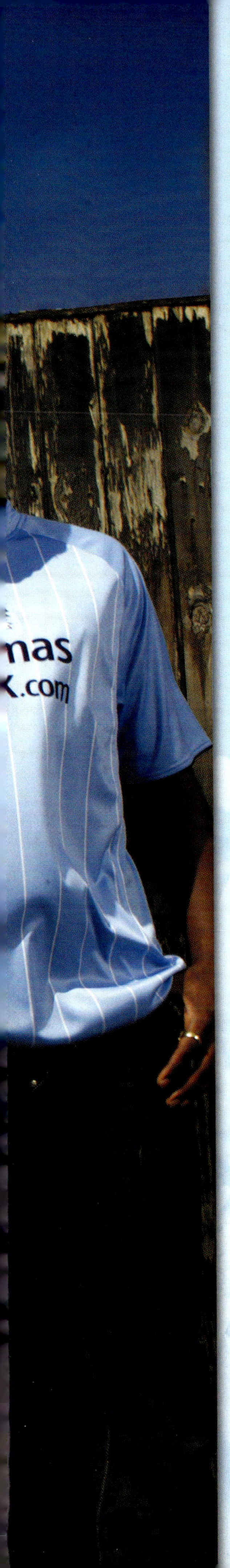

The Story of the 2006/07 Season

STUART PEARCE brought several new faces into the team for the 2006/07 season, including Italian striker Bernardo Corradi, French midfielder Ousmane Dabo, German anchorman Dietmar Hamann, striker Paul Dickov, utility man Hatem Trabelsi and DaMarcus Beasley – an American winger on loan from PSV Eindhoven.

The Blues drew the short straw by having to face Premiership title-holders Chelsea at Stamford Bridge on the opening day of the new campaign, a team that rarely drop points at home, though the 3-0 win still flattered them, somewhat. Corradi was sent off on his debut to complete a miserable afternoon in West London.

Portsmouth were the first visitors to the City of Manchester Stadium and left with a 0-0 draw, though Ben Thatcher's nasty challenge on Pompey's Pedro Mendes made most of the headlines. Arsenal were next to visit SportCity and a Joey Barton penalty was enough to give the Blues a rare victory over Arsene Wenger's side.

City dominated the next game, away to Reading, but still lost 1-0 and again had a player harshly sent off, this time Ousmane Dabo and six days later a 4-2 defeat at Blackburn left the Blues pointless from their three away trips – and there was worse to follow when City crashed out of the Carling Cup to League One side Chesterfield.

A win was desperately needed to boost confidence and thanks to two excellent Georgios Samaras goals, they got it in the form of a 2-0 win over West Ham. It took an injury-time equaliser from Micah Richards to take a first point away from home in a 1-1 draw at Everton, but it was followed by a disappointing home 0-0 draw with Sheffield United – goals were clearly a problem for Pearce's side who slipped to 12th place following an awful display at Wigan, who scored four times without reply during the Blues' worst display of the season.

With bogey side Middlesbrough next up at home, nothing but a win would do for the anxious home support and a Richard Dunne header would prove enough to take all three points. Just one point and no goals from the next two games (Charlton away, Newcastle home) meant the Blues had failed to score in seven of the 11 Premiership matches played, though the form at the City of Manchester Stadium was exemplary, having still not conceded a single goal in six games!

Fulham were beaten by half-time and the Blues' fans had something to cheer. Two goals from Corradi and another from Barton paved the way for a 3-1 home win. A narrow defeat at Liverpool was followed by a terrific 3-1 win away to Aston Villa, with Sylvain Distin scoring a fine solo goal ending a miserable run of away results and with bottom club Watford next on the agenda at the CoMS, there was a real chance to put a good run together. It proved to be a frustrating evening, however, as the visitors left with a deserved 0-0 draw – the fourth scoreless draw out of eight home games.

With three tough fixtures coming up against Manchester United away, and then home to two sides who'd both won on their last two visits to CoMS – Bolton and Spurs - City needed to raise their performance levels in order to take any points, but the Blues lost all three, adding yet more pressure on the manager and team as they prepared for the busy festive period.

The Story of the 2006/07 Season (Cont...)

It was now crucial that defeat was avoided in the next two matches at Sheffield United and West Ham and in a classic smash and grab raid, the Blues won both games 1-0 with late winners. Two Samaras goals on New Year's Day gave City a 2-1 win over Everton and a third win on the trot – though nobody would ever have guessed those would be the last Premiership goals scored at home that season – especially with eight games still to play on home turf!

Michael Ball and Emile Mpenza were added to the squad in early 2007, though Claudio Reyna and Ben Thatcher left for pastures new. At least the FA Cup provided a welcome distraction and Sheffield Wednesday were dispatched 2-1 after a replay (the first match ending 1-1). Despite just one point from the clashes with Bolton and Blackburn, a 3-1 win over Southampton in the fourth round of the FA Cup put Pearce's men into the last 16 with another Championship side to face in round five in the shape of Preston North End. Defeats at home to Reading (0-2) and at Portsmouth (1-2) were sandwiched in between, but the Blues comfortably dispatched Preston at Deepdale to go into the quarter-finals for a second successive year and everyone wondered, 'Is it our year?'

Yet the team couldn't take their Cup form into the Premiership and Wigan became the third successive side to leave the Blues' home ground with maximum points. It seemed the whole season now hinged on an FA Cup sixth round trip to Blackburn Rovers. More than 7,000 City fans travelled to Ewood Park in good spirits, but it was to be another disappointing afternoon, as City fell behind to a rather fortuitous goal early on. Despite having much of the play and seeing the hosts reduced to 10 men, the Blues hardly managed a shot on goal and Rovers added a second late on, sparking angry scenes from

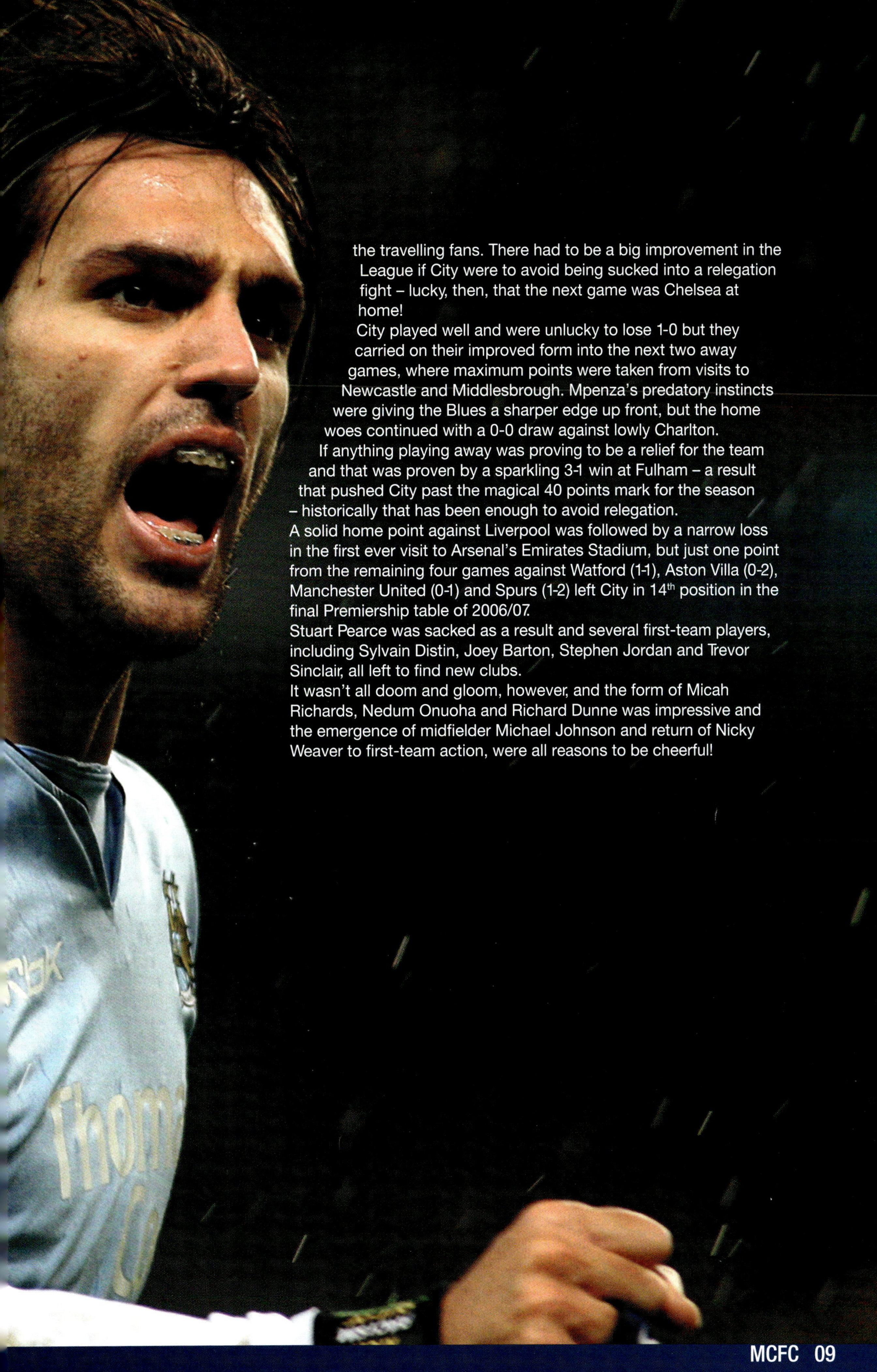

the travelling fans. There had to be a big improvement in the League if City were to avoid being sucked into a relegation fight – lucky, then, that the next game was Chelsea at home!

City played well and were unlucky to lose 1-0 but they carried on their improved form into the next two away games, where maximum points were taken from visits to Newcastle and Middlesbrough. Mpenza's predatory instincts were giving the Blues a sharper edge up front, but the home woes continued with a 0-0 draw against lowly Charlton.

If anything playing away was proving to be a relief for the team and that was proven by a sparkling 3-1 win at Fulham – a result that pushed City past the magical 40 points mark for the season – historically that has been enough to avoid relegation.

A solid home point against Liverpool was followed by a narrow loss in the first ever visit to Arsenal's Emirates Stadium, but just one point from the remaining four games against Watford (1-1), Aston Villa (0-2), Manchester United (0-1) and Spurs (1-2) left City in 14th position in the final Premiership table of 2006/07.

Stuart Pearce was sacked as a result and several first-team players, including Sylvain Distin, Joey Barton, Stephen Jordan and Trevor Sinclair, all left to find new clubs.

It wasn't all doom and gloom, however, and the form of Micah Richards, Nedum Onuoha and Richard Dunne was impressive and the emergence of midfielder Michael Johnson and return of Nicky Weaver to first-team action, were all reasons to be cheerful!

Here are five of the best goals scored during the 2006/07 campaign ...

GOAL! Georgios Samaras

v West Ham 23/9/06

This was a goal made by the pace and power of Ishmael Miller who picked up the ball on the edge of his own box, shook off two challenges and then began to run towards the West Ham box. His momentum carried him past one more defender before he drove a shot into a defender. The resulting deflection went to Georgios Samaras on the edge of the box who controlled the ball on his chest and then powered home an unstoppable volley from 18 yards.

GOAL! Micah Richards

v Everton 30/9/06

As we all know, Micah only scores his goals in injury time – the 94th minute to be precise and this goal at Goodison Park preserved that record. Chasing an equaliser with just seconds left, Sylvain Distin hoofed the ball forward to Bernardo Corradi who flicked the ball on for Micah to hammer home a volley from close range off the underside of the bar to cue wild celebrations on and off the pitch.

GOAL! Bernardo Corradi

v Portsmouth 10/2/07

Bernardo Corradi showed what a threat he can be given the right service when he scored only his third goal for the Blues at Fratton Park. Sun Jihai won the ball for City and fed Joey Barton, who then found Darius Vassell out on the right. Vassell swung over a perfect cross towards Corradi who glanced a delightful header past David James.

GOAL! Michael Ball

v Preston 18/2/07

The Blues were 1-0 down to Preston at a critical stage of the first half. City had the momentum but needed an equaliser and on 35 minutes, they got their just reward. A fine move involving Barton and Trabelsi saw the Tunisian utility man pick out Bernardo Corradi who spun well and hit the post with a stunning volley. The rebound fell kindly to Michael Ball who controlled the ball before firing a fierce drive high in off the post for his first City goal.

GOAL! Emile Mpenza

v Middlesbrough 17/3/07

This was a goal scored by sheer guts and endeavour by Belgian striker Emile Mpenza. His first goal in City colours came as the Blues looked to seal a first win at the Riverside Stadium. Leading 1-0 through Distin's close-range effort, City were bossing the play and when Lee Cattermole was dispossessed by Joey Barton who fed the ball into Mpenza's path. He held off one challenge before sliding the ball past Mark Schwarzer which went in off a post before rolling into the net to seal the victory.

BEST GOAL !

Colin Bell Stan
RBK
BARCLAYS
PREMIERSHIP
Thomas
Cook

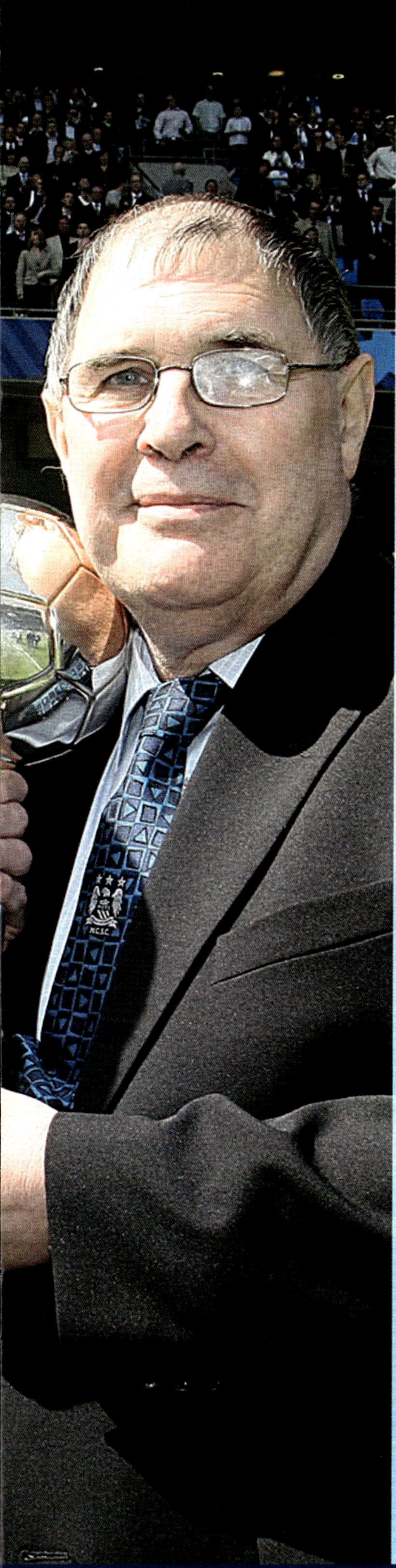

Richard Dunne

City captain Richard Dunne picked up his third successive Player of the Year award when he was voted the runaway winner at the end of the 2006/07 campaign. The Republic of Ireland international was the only player to have played every minute of every Premiership game for City last season and he was an inspirational figure throughout. Brave, determined and hard-working, Dunne is the perfect example of everything a captain should be and he became the first City player to ever win the Player of the Year award three times in a row and only the second player to win a hat-trick of awards (the other being Joe Corrigan). Dunne joined City from Everton in 2000 at a cost of £3.5m and only Nicky Weaver has been at the club longer. On receiving his award, the Blues' skipper said: "It's a great personal achievement being voted Player of the Year by our own fans who watch us every week is what really counts for me. As long as I'm doing right by our fans, that's good enough for me."

Dunne Factfile:

BORN:
21/9/79
BIRTHPLACE:
Dublin
HEIGHT:
6' 2"
NICKNAME:
Dunney
SQUAD NUMBER:
22
FORMER CLUBS:
Home Farm (schoolboy), Everton
HIS MATES SAY:
"Ever since I've come to this club Richard has just been quality. I play with him week in, week out and I think he's one of the best players I've played with. I've played with John Terry and Rio Ferdinand in the England squad but Richard is right up there with them." – Micah Richards
DID YOU KNOW?
Richard named his daughter Lyla after an Oasis song – Oasis are his favourite band

MicahRichards

Micah Richards rounded off a fantastic year by being voted City's Young Player of the Year 2007 for the second successive year. Micah was also nominated for the PFA Young Player of the Year and was on a shortlist of six youngsters that included Cristiano Ronaldo, Cesc Fabregas, Wayne Rooney and Aaron Lennon. It was an amazing 12 months for Micah who moved from the Academy Under 18s into the reserves effortlessly to become one of the brightest prospects the club has produced in years – and there's been a few! Strong, quick and intelligent, Micah has become a firm favourite among the City supporters and he became the second Academy graduate to play for England in 2006 when he made his debut against Holland, adding three more caps last season. He also became the youngest defender to ever play for England – quite an achievement!

Micah said: "To be voted Young Player of the Year by City fans was fantastic. I'm aiming for the main award next year, if Dunney will give someone else a chance!"

Micah Factfile:

BORN:
24/6/88
BIRTHPLACE:
Birmingham
HEIGHT:
5' 11"
NICKNAME:
Meeks
SQUAD NUMBER:
2
FORMER CLUBS:
Oldham Athletic (schoolboy)
HIS MATES SAY:
"Micah has done brilliantly in 2006/07. Now he's playing for England he's probably our biggest name." - Richard Dunne
DID YOU KNOW?
Micah supported Arsenal as a boy and his hobby is deejaying. His only two career goals up to the start of the 2007/08 season were injury time equalisers at Aston Villa and Everton, respectively.

Ched Evans Factfile:

Born: 28/12/88
Birthplace: Rhyl
Height: 6'0"
Former clubs: Academy graduate
His mates say: Ched is a practical joker!

ChedEvans

Ched Evans was voted City's Most Promising Player of the Year for 2007 after finishing top scorer for the Under-18 side and also making excellent progress in the reserves. He capped off a memorable season by winning his first cap for Wales Under-21s, scoring twice on his debut against Northern Ireland. The Rhyl-born teenager is an old-fashioned striker – powerful in the air and a good finisher and his exploits last season won him a two-year deal with which he hopes to make an impression on the first-team squad.

Ched said: "I feel more confident and that my game is improving all the time. I've been training at Carrington for a while now and obviously I'll be looking to push on again next season.

"I didn't have a clue that I'd been voted Most Promising Player by the supporters - at first I thought it was an award from the Academy coaches or something! That it actually came from the City fans is even better. I'd like to be in or around the first-team by September 2007 and if I get my chance, I aim to take it, like Micah did."

Position: Goalkeeper
Date of birth: 3/10/81
Place of birth: Trelleborg
Height: 6' 6"
Previous clubs: Trelleborg, Juventus, Djurgardens, Rennes,
Signed: Aug 06
Fee: £2m

Position: Goalkeeper
Date of birth: 19/4/87
Place of birth: Shrewsbury
Height: 6' 5"
Previous clubs: Shrewsbury Town, Blackpool (loan), Tranmere (loan)
Signed: May 06
Fee: £600,000

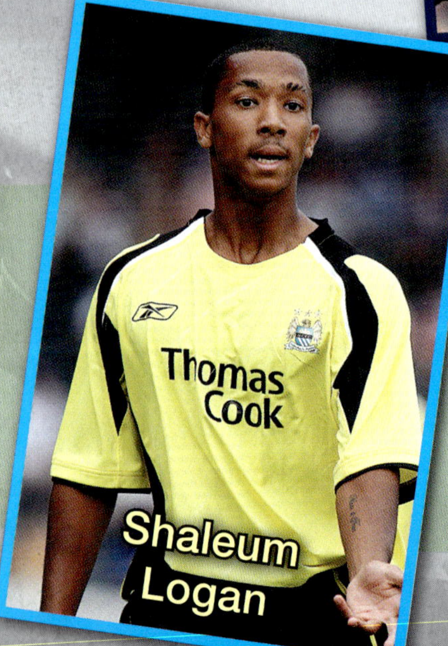

Position: Defender
Date of birth: 29/01/88
Place of birth: Manchester
Height: 5' 8"
Previous clubs: None,
Signed: Academy
Fee: NONE

Position: Goalkeeper
Date of birth: 5/11/86
Place of birth: Denmark
Height: 6' 1"
Previous clubs: Darlington (loan), Bury (loan), Falkirk (loan)
Signed: Academy
Fee: NONE

Position: Central defence
Date of birth: 21/9/79
Place of birth: Dublin, Ireland
Height: 6' 2"
Previous clubs: Everton
Signed: October 2000
Fee: £3m

Position: Defender
Date of birth: 14/7/86
Place of birth: Swindon
Height: 6' 3"
Previous clubs: Southampton, Coventry (loan), Colchester (loan), Bournemouth (loan)
Signed: Jan 06
Fee: £250,000

Michael Ball

Position: Full-back
Date of birth: 2/10/79
Place of birth: Liverpool
Height: 5' 10"
Previous clubs: Everton, Rangers, PSV Eindhoven
Signed: Jan 2007
Fee: Undisclosed

Michael Johnson

Position: Midfield
Date of birth: 24/2/88
Place of birth: Manchester
Height: 6' 0"
Previous clubs: None
Signed: Academy graduate
Fee: None

Nedum Onuoha

Position: Defender
Date of birth: 12/11/86
Place of birth: Warri, Nigeria
Height: 6' 0"
Previous clubs: None
Signed: Academy
Fee: None

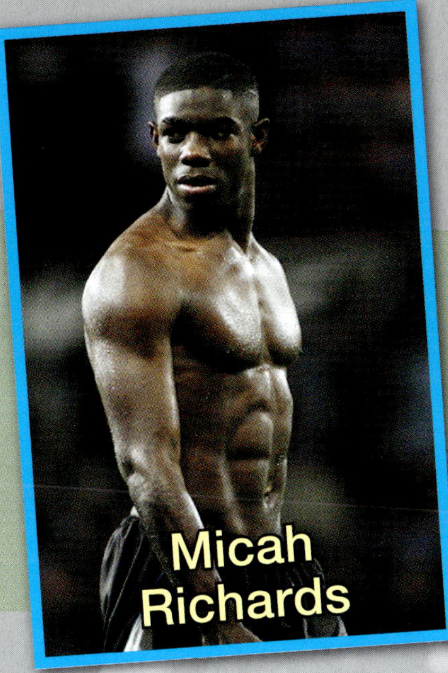

Micah Richards

Position: Defender/ Midfielder
Date of birth: 24/6/1988
Place of birth: Birmingham
Height: 5' 11"
Previous clubs: Oldham (youth)
Signed: Academy
Fee: NONE

Sun Jihai

Position: Defender
Date of birth: 30/9/1977
Place of birth: Dalian, China
Height: 5' 9"
Previous clubs: Dalian Wanda, Crystal Palace
Signed: Feb 02
Fee: £2m

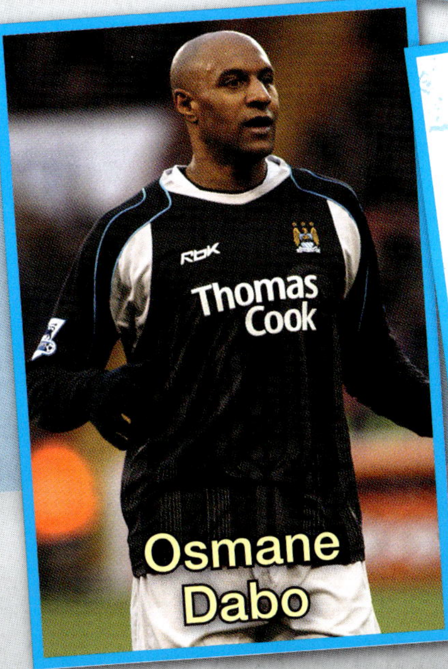

Osmane Dabo

Position: Midfielder
Date of birth: 8/2/1977
Place of birth: Laval, France
Height: 6' 1"
Previous clubs: Rennes, Vicenza, Atalanta, Monaco, Parma, Inter Milan, Lazio
Signed: June 2006
Fee: Free

Stephen Ireland

Position: Midfielder
Date of birth: 22/8/1986
Place of birth: Cork, Ireland
Height: 5' 8"
Previous clubs: None
Signed: Academy
Fee: NONE

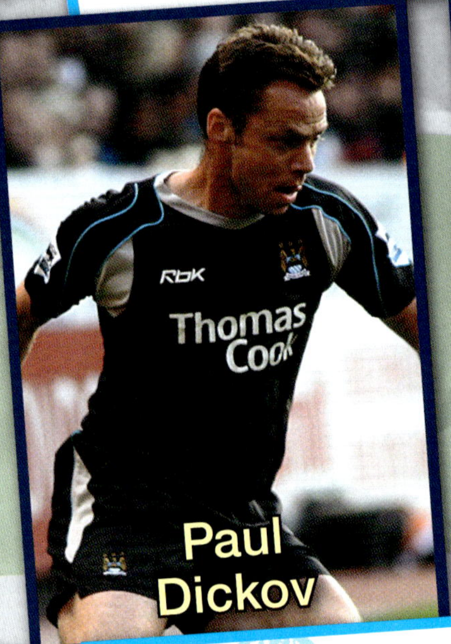

Paul Dickov

Position: Striker
Date of birth: 1/11/1972
Place of birth: Livingston, Scotland
Height: 5' 6"
Previous clubs: Arsenal, Brighton (loan), Leicester, Blackburn
Signed: May 2006
Fee: Free

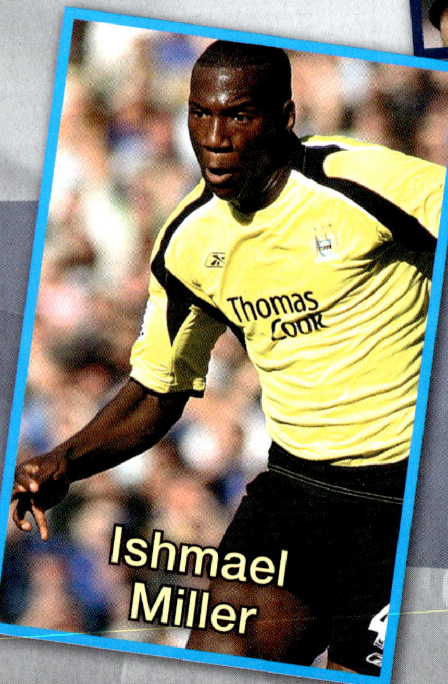

Ishmael Miller

Position: Striker
Date of birth: 5/3/87
Place of birth: Manchester
Height: 6' 3"
Previous clubs: None
Signed: Academy
Fee: NONE

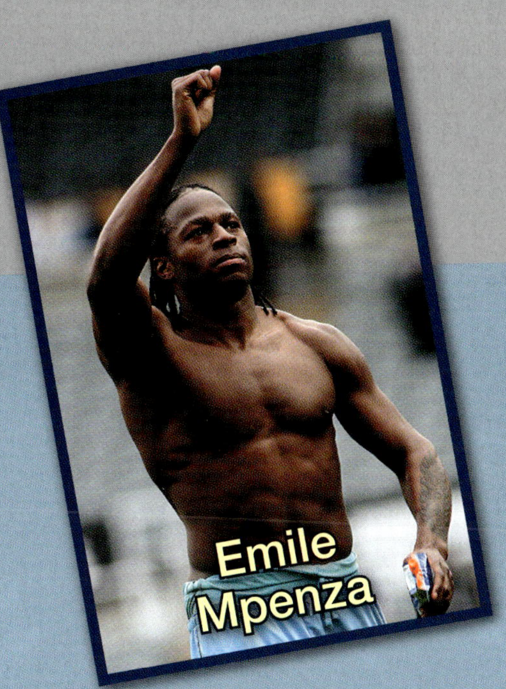

Emile
Mpenza

Position: Striker
Date of birth: 4/7/78
Place of birth:
Zellik, Belgium
Height: 5' 10"
Previous clubs:
Standard Liege, SV
Hamburg, Schalke 04,
Al-Rayaan
Signed: 16/2/07
Fee: Free

Georgios
Samaras

Position: Striker
Date of birth: 21/2/85
Place of birth:
Heraklion, Greece
Height: 6' 4"
Previous clubs:
Heerenveen
Signed: Jan 2006
Fee: £6m

Darius
Vassell

Position: Striker
Date of birth: 30/6/80
Place of birth:
Birmingham
Height: 5' 9"
Previous clubs:
Aston Villa
Signed: July 2005
Fee: £2m

Born: Cobh, Ireland, 22/08/86.

Position: Centre midfield.

Nickname: 'Tally' – I really haven't a clue why – I don't think my friends know either.

Team supported: Manchester United until I arrived at City aged 14 and everything changed.

Clubs played for: Cobh Ramblers and Manchester City.

Strengths: I love going forward with the ball and attacking.

Heroes: Eric Cantona, Ronaldinho and Zinedine Zidane.

I play a bit like... A few people at the club have said I remind them a bit of Eyal Berkovic. I love playing from box-to-box and defending as well but my main trait is going forward.

High: Getting through into City's first team. I never thought my chance would come so quickly and never thought I'd achieve what I have so far. Scoring the first ever goal for the Republic of Ireland at the Croke Park Stadium will take some beating, too. Now I need to be consistent and prove myself.

Low: Breaking my wrist against Olympiakos in a pre-season friendly.

Toughest opponent: West Ham's left-winger, Matthew Etherington has been my toughest opponent so far. Doriva of Middlesbrough was difficult for half a game, too.

Best player played with: All the lads in City's first team plus the Academy lads I played alongside for four years.

Biggest influence: There's been are a lot of inspiring people at the club including coaches Steve Wigley, Juan Carlos Osorio and Stuart Pearce, who I'll always be grateful for giving me my chance.

Tunes: I'm a huge Robbie Williams fan and I also love R & B music, particularly Jagged Edge, 50 Cent and One-Twelve.

Wheels: I'm still struggling to drive – if you ask me the same question in 10 years I still won't be driving. I just can't drive and even when I've booked in lessons the football seems to get in the way and I just can't be bothered. I'm way too lazy!

Films: I love movies, especially horror films but I get very scared when I watch them. I like action movies and comedies, too.

I laugh at: Billy Connolly – I just love him and I'm his biggest fan ever, I've never seen him live and I'm waiting for his next UK tour.

Holiday destination: I spent four nights in Marbella with my family and it was brilliant. It was the first time we went away as a family together and I loved it so that's going to take some beating.

If I hadn't been a footballer... I'd be really struggling and I haven't a clue what I'd be doing. I've dedicated myself to football and I've never considered anything else.

In five years time I'll be... hopefully saying I'm enjoying my sixth season in the first team for City and still playing regular international football for Ireland. I could have qualified to play for England, Ireland or Italy if I'd have wanted to.

MoonieCrossword

Moonchester has created a crossword that you'll need all your knowledge on City to solve. Answer the questions, fill in the blanks and see if you can complete the puzzle.

ACROSS

2 Surname of player who got sent off on his debut last season (7)
3 City's England Under-21 'keeper (3,4)
4 Name of Stuart Pearce's lucky horse mascot (6)
7 DaMarcus, who spent last season on loan at City (7)
8 Richard Dunne's city of birth (6)
13 Club Bernardo Corradi joined from (8)
15 Club that knocked Blues out of Carling Cup in 2006/7 (12)
16 Location of City of Manchester's Stadium (9)
18 Surname of last player to score a home goal in 2006/7 campaign (7)
19 Club Sylvain Distin joined last summer (10)

DOWN

1 Name of City's training complex (10)
2 Jihai Sun's nationality (7)
5 Team that knocked Blues out of 2006/7 FA Cup (9)
6 Andreas Isaksson played for this Italian club (8)
9 City's Academy is based here (5,4)
10 City where Micah Richards was born (10)
11 Scottish side Kasper Schmeichel went on loan to in 2006/7 (7)
12 Country of Nedum Onuoha's birth (7)
14 Christian name of player who missed a penalty against Manchester United in May 2007 (6)
17 Name of Kasper Schmeichel's famous father (5)

The Boss

Sven-Goran Eriksson became City's new manager in early July. Here, we look at the man aiming to make the Blues a force to be reckoned with

WHEN it comes to managing football clubs, Sven-Goran Eriksson knows his stuff. In fact, his record is almost unsurpassed having had success virtually wherever he's gone. His spell as England manager was also, by comparison with previous managers, one of the most successful reigns as national team boss so the Blues have employed a man with a terrific track record. But what about Sven's background?

Well, he was born on February 5, 1948 in the small Swedish town of Torsby, which has a population of approximately 4,000.

Sven's love of football led to a modest career in the lower leagues of Swedish football before a knee injury ended his playing days when he was aged only 27. Determined not to drift out of the game, he moved into coaching and, in 1976, he took on his first role as coach of Degerfors IF A year later he became their manager – his first managerial role and he proved to be an instant hit, taking the club from the third division to the first in just three years.

His achievements didn't go unnoticed by bigger Swedish clubs and he became manager of IFK Gothenburg, and steered his new team to victory in the Swedish Cup in his first year in charge. Sven then became a legendary figure among IFK supporters when he not only won the league and cup in 1982, but completed an unprecedented treble by winning the UEFA Cup as well! Not a bad start to a managerial career!

The humble, quiet man from Torsby was suddenly one of the hottest managerial talents in Europe and the lure of proving himself on foreign soil was too big a pull for the ambitious 33-year-old and he accepted Benfica's offer to become their manager. Would the change of scenery and style of football affect his progress? Well only if you count another domestic double as failure as he guided Benfica to the Portuguese Championship, the Portuguese Cup as well as finishing runners-up in the UEFA Cup – all within a year of taking charge. Everything Sven touched turned to gold.

Benfica were crowned league champions the following season and during the summer he moved to Italy to become manager of AS Roma. In his second year in Serie A, Roma lifted the coveted Coppa Italia and Sven was again a wanted man, this time by rivals Fiorentina, though his two years there would prove to be the least successful of his career – at least by his standards – and he left the club having won no trophies and instead returned to Benfica for a second spell as their manager.

Sven picked up where he'd left off by taking Benfica to the 1990 European Cup final (now Champions League final), and then won the league a year later. To Benfica fans, Sven was a God, so there was great disappointment when he left for Sampdoria in 1992 for a second crack at Italian football.

In 1994 he enjoyed his second Coppa Italia success before taking charge of his fourth Italian club by becoming boss at Lazio in 1997 – it would be the beginning of the most successful spell of his career so far, with a string of triumphs with the Roman giants. After one year in charge they lifted the Italian Cup and the Italian Super Cup and in 1999 he oversaw a unique European double by winning the European Cup Winners' Cup and the UEFA Super Cup before he landed the trophy he'd most coveted in 2000 as Lazio were crowned champions of Serie A.

No wonder England identified him as the outstanding candidate to become the new national team manager in 2001 and when he accepted the role, he became England's first foreign coach. He would become the third longest serving manager behind legendary figures Sir Alf Ramsey and Sir Bobby Robson, he spent 67 matches in charge. His record in major tournaments – just three defeats in 38 games, 26 of which ended in victory, is excellent, though Sven's thoughtful, calm pitch-side manner actually attracted criticism in some quarters. Ranting and raving has never been his style, though, and with the success he's had over the years, why should he change now?

On accepting the position, Sven said: "I am absolutely delighted and honoured to have been asked to be Manchester City's manager. This is an exciting challenge and I want to deliver a team that our fantastic fans can be proud of."

Michael
Johnson

Emile
Empenza

Can you spot the ball?

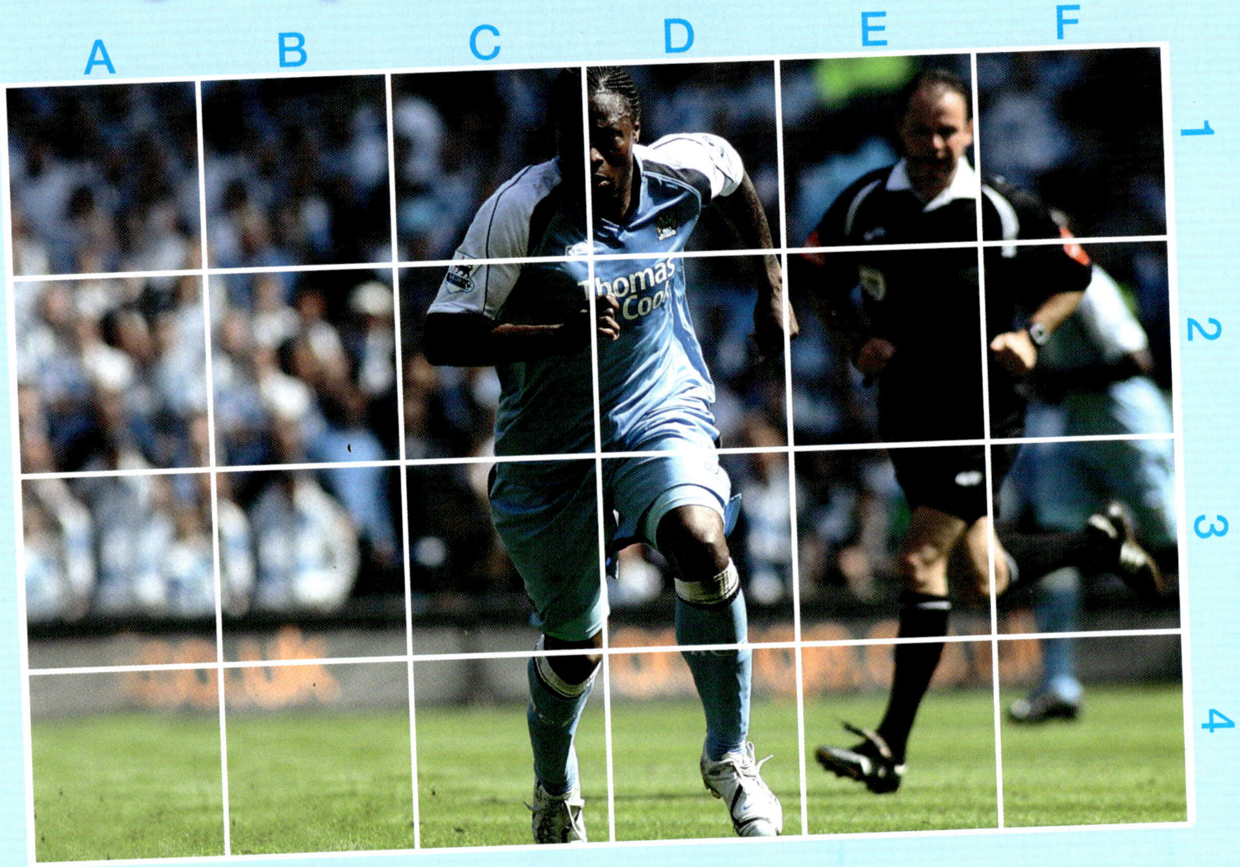

Answers on page 60/61

GuessWho?

Which players are hidden here, do you know your stuff?

A

B

C

D

Answers on page 60/61

Petrov Wings In!

FLYING winger Martin Petrov signed for City during the summer at a cost of £4.7m from Spanish side Atletico Madrid. Petrov, 28, is a Bulgarian international who will add pace and width to the Blues' attack – something the team lacked last season and the left-sided midfielder turned down a chance to link up with his international colleague Dimitar Berbatov at Tottenham. Petrov was voted Bulgaria's footballer of the year in 2006 and has played for CSKA Sofia, Servette, Wolfsburg, and Atletico Madrid. He can score and create goals and has earned 64 caps for his country. The attraction of playing under Sven-Goran Eriksson proved too great for Petrov, who signed a three-year deal with City.

"The main reason I joined Manchester City was because of the manager," said Petrov, who was born on January 15,

1979 in the Bulgarian town of Vratsa.
He began his career for CSKA Sofia, where he was soon dubbed 'the new Hristo Stoitchkov' – a Bulgarian legend. After two impressive displays against Servette in the UEFA Cup for CSKA, the Swiss side decided to buy the powerful 19-year-old and he remained in Switzerland for three years, making 75 appearances and scoring 22 goals. While with Servette, he made his national team debut against England, but it was a game memorable for all the wrong reasons after he was shown the red card! In 2001 he moved to the German Bundesliga and established himself as an explosive talented player for VfL Wolfsburg. He became a firm favourite with the supporters during his four years with the club, playing 116 times and scoring 28 goals. In the summer of 2005 he was bought by Atlético Madrid for approximately £7.5m. Petrov was Bulgaria's best player during Euro 2004, shining in the three games his country played and scoring their only goal during a 2-1 defeat to Italy. His performances in 2006 earned him the Bulgarian Footballer of the Year award, amid stiff competition from the likes of Berbatov and Aston Villa's Stilian Petrov (no relation to Martin!)

A penalty expert and capable of scoring goals out of nothing, Petrov, a physical and very fast winger should prove to be a massive hit with City fans during the 2007/08 season.

Born: Urmston, Manchester, 24/2/88.

Position: Centre midfield.

Nickname: 'Johnno' for obvious reasons!

Team supported: Leeds United – my dad supported them I sort of just inherited them. I'm not even sure why I supported them, come to think of it…

Clubs played for: Manchester City.

Strengths: Passing.

Weaknesses: I could head it better and I could score more goals.

Heroes: Zinedine Zidane.

I play a bit like… I'd like to have aspects of Steven Gerrard, Owen Hargreaves and Frank Lampard's game.

High: Playing against Manchester United in my first Manchester derby – the result was wrong but I enjoyed the occasion. Playing Arsenal at the Emirates Stadium and setting up our goal was special, too.

Low: Making my debut at Wigan and losing 4-0. I cracked a bone in my wrist that day, just for good measure.

Toughest opponent: Nicky Butt, Newcastle.

Best player played with: Richard Dunne - a colossus.

Biggest practical joker: Ben Thatcher.

Biggest influence on career: My dad – he's been with me all the way over the years.

Best advice given: Don't play the ball across your own area, like I did at Newcastle!

Wheels: Ford Explorer.

TV programmes: I don't like staying in and watching TV. I'd rather go out.

Most embarrassing moment: It was a couple of years ago when I was doing my college day as an Academy player. I was getting a tenner out of the cash till when one of the lads ran up behind and whipped my tracksuit bottoms down. I didn't do anything, just finished getting my money and calmly pulled them back up.

Holiday destination: I love travelling and there are too many places I want to go to name just one.

If I hadn't been a footballer… I would probably be working as a car salesman at my dad's garage.

With my first pay packet I… Paid some bills.

If I could play alongside one player it would be: Zinedine Zidane.

In five years' time I'd like to be… Playing regularly for City in the Premiership and playing for England.

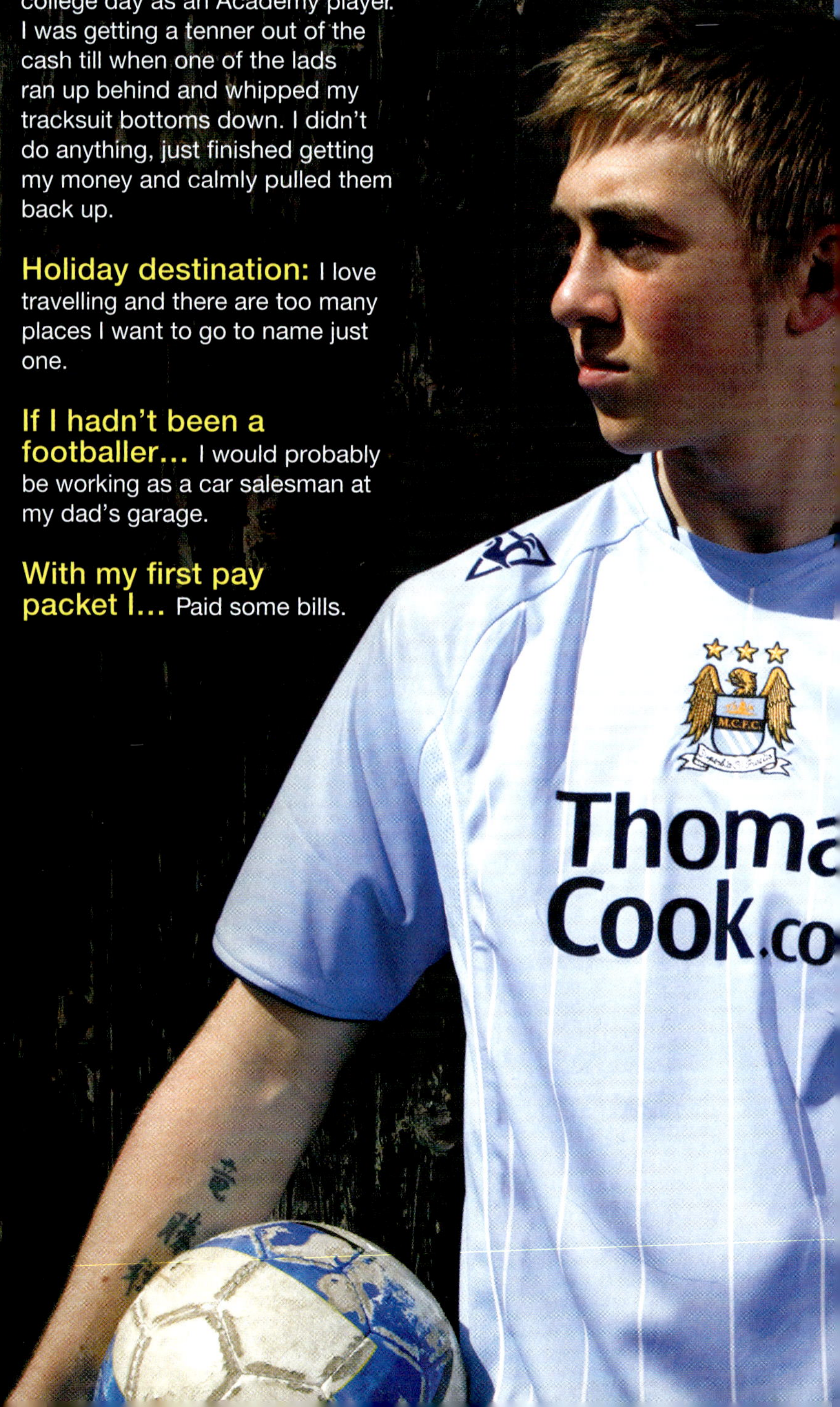

Talkagoodgame?

Below is a section of fictional commentary based on a real game – you've got to fill in the missing words by working out which match we're talking about and who the missing players are!

1) "______________ ______________ picks up the ball on the edge of his own area. He moves it out to the left and powers down the line. The West ham defenders can't catch him! He's like a runaway freight train – he checks inside, fires a shot, it comes out to ______________ ______________ who chests it up, volleys it and – oh, what a goal!"

2) "City still trail 1-0. The ball is played out to ______________ ______________ ______________ who gets the ball, looks up and whips in a cross to ______________ ______________ who glances the ball past David James for 1-1 – terrific header!"

3) "This has to be the last chance, here comes the ball into the Everton box, flicked on by ______________ ______________ to ______________ ______________ - and what a fantastic volley by the youngster – what was he doing up there? Ten out of ten for the cartwheel, too!"

4) "______________ ______________ was tripped in the box and ______________ ______________ ______________ now has a chance to equalise for City from the penalty spot. Ten minutes left, here he goes – oh the keeper has saved! City still trail 1-0."

5) "City keep the pressure on their Championship opponents. ______________ ______________, out on the right, chips it into ______________ ______________ who spins and crashed the ball off the bar! So close! The rebound falls to ______________ ______________ - what a goal! In off the post to level the scores!"

Answers on page 60/61

There's Only One Rolando!

ROLANDO BIANCHI became Sven-Goran Eriksson's first signing when he paid Italian side Reggina approximately £8.8m to bring the 24-year-old striker to Manchester.

Bianchi's 18 goals put him fourth on the list of Serie A top scorers last season and his goals helped keep Reggina in the top flight. The former Atalanta and Cagliari forward is one of the most highly regarded up and coming talents in Italian football and the City boss was delighted to bring Bianchi to City.

"He scored nearly 20 goals last season in Serie A, which is a lot of goals in such a difficult league," said Sven. "He's young, and I think it's a very important signing because he should have a great future. He's a good footballer as well as a good goalscorer, which is what we need.

"He's very hard working, very strong and he can score - if you can score nearly 20 goals in Serie A and you are not with one of the top clubs like Milan or Juve then you must be talented. It's a good record, and let's hope he continues with it."

Bianchi became the second most expensive player in the club's history and the striker reckons he can become a big hit with the City fans in his first year.

"I know that it will take time and hard work for me to adapt to playing in England, but that will not be a problem.

"If people feel that Italian players have not always been successful in the Premiership - and I don't think that is the case - then I aim to be the exception. I speak enough English to understand some things, but it is vital for me to take lessons. Sven was important in my decision to come here. He talked to me a lot on the phone. I respect him greatly as a coach and he sold me his vision for City's future. It is going to be very exciting.

"My team-mate Bernardo Corradi told me not to think about the differences between English and Italian football and just to be myself and be confident that I can do well here.

"In my early career I was quite strong in the air but I have improved all aspects of my game. I enjoy the physical side, but I feel I can adapt to any style whether that be a direct one or a more technical one."

Bianchi, who was born in Port-De-Bouc, Bergamo on February 15, 1983, has represented his country at Under-21 level, winning 13 caps and scoring 7 goals. He began his career with Atalanta aged 18 after being a prolific scorer for the reserves, and played 21 times before being loaned to Serie B side Cagliari and played 39 times during his stay.

He was then transferred to Reggina in 2005, but played only nine times in his first season after sustaining a knee injury for the Under-21s. He returned in 2006 and took Serie A by storm by scoring 18 goals in a struggling side. With flying winger Martin Petrov supplying the ammunition, Rolando is hoping to be an instant hit with the City fans.

M.C.F.C.
BIANCHI
10

Stephen
Ireland
Thomas
Cook

MoonieMaze
Moonchester has to make the trip to SportCity from his home on the moon - can you help him find his way?
MCFC 39

LIVE4CITY
jnr blues
Thomas Cook
Colour In Moonbeam...
40 MCFC

LIVE4CITY
M.C.F.C.
Superbia In Proelio
LIVE4CITY
FREE MEMBERSHIP AND DISCOUNTED HOME MATCH TICKETS
IT'S FREE TO EVERYONE UNDER THE AGE OF 16
FREE MEMBERSHIP
ALL UNDER 16s SIGN UP NOW
WWW.LIVE4CITY.CO.UK

GetTheMessage?

Here are four mobile phones with text messages on – work out who is sending the message and fill in the blanks

Can you spot the difference?

There are ten items found in picture **A** that have been taken out of picture **B**, can you find them all?

Answers on page 60/61

Here is a detailed aerial image of City's training facility at Carrington

All-weather 5-a-side pitch
Player and staff car park
Carrington Complex Key Guide
Medical Department
Doctor's office & waiting room/ hydropool
Gymnasium
Canteen/players rest area (upper level)
Changing rooms/boot room/showers
Manager's office
Main reception
Administrative offices
Laundry room/ kit room
Groundstaff offices/storage facility

The Manchester derby is one of the most eagerly awaited fixtures in English football – here are two pages packed with derby day facts and figures

Derby Day Fact 1:

The first Manchester derby took place on October 3, 1891 when Newton Heath beat Ardwick 5-1 during an FA Cup first round qualifier. Newton Heath later became Manchester United and Ardwick became Manchester City.

Derby Day Fact 2:

The first competitive fixture the teams played as Manchester City v Manchester United was on Christmas Day, 1902 when a record crowd of 40,000 witnessed a 1-1 draw at Newton Heath and the Reds won the return fixture at Hyde Road, then City's home ground, 2-0.

Derby Day Fact 3:

City had to wait until December 1, 1906 to record a first league win over Manchester United, with a 3-0 win delighting the 30,000 Hyde Road crowd.

Derby Day Fact 4:

Former Manchester United striker Denis Law scored the goal that gave the Blues a 1-0 win at Old Trafford and confirmed United's relegation in 1974.

Derby Day Fact 5:

City and United have met three times in the League Cup, with the Blues unbeaten in all three matches. United have the edge in the FA Cup meetings, winning five to City's two.

Derby Day Fact 6:

City beat United 6-1 at Old Trafford in 1926 – the biggest ever derby victory. Two goals each for Austin and Roberts plus strikes from Johnson and Hicks secured the victory in front of nearly 50,000 fans. Despite such a stunning win, the Blues were relegated at the end of the season! City also won 5-0 at Old Trafford in 1955.

The complete record is (to 01/08/07):

League	Pld	W	D	L	F	A
City	136	35	48	53	181	198
United	136	53	48	35	198	181

FA Cup	Pld	W	D	L	F	A
City	7	2	0	5	5	9
United	7	5	0	2	9	5

League Cup	Pld	W	D	L	F	A
City	3	2	1	0	8	3
United	3	0	1	2	3	8

Totals:	Pld	W	D	L	F	A
City	147	39	49	59	194	211
United	147	59	49	39	211	194

Trivia: The City of Manchester Stadium is 4.7 miles from Old Trafford whereas City's old ground Maine Road was only 3.3 miles away.

Andreas
Isaksson

Moonbeam's Rock Cakes

Here's a special recipe Moonbeam has cooked up for you - it's what Moonchester likes best after he's eaten all his dinner up! You'll need a grown-up to help you do this so don't try it on your own because it involves a hot oven!

Ingredients

– to make about 24 Moonie rock cakes:

300g plain flour
100g butter
100g sugar
½ cup raisins
1 egg
Blue food colouring
(this is optional)

Method:

Ask a grown-up to turn the oven on to 200 C/ 400 F /gas mark 6 and make sure you've got a lightly greased baking tray ready. You can grease the tray if it's OK!
Tip the flour into a large mixing bowl and then add the butter. This is where it gets messy – hurrah! Using your fingers, crumble the butter into the flour. This may take a few minutes and the mixture will then start to turn into fine crumbs. When you are happy with your mixture, add the sugar and then the raisins – you can eat one raisin now if you're really, really hungry! Mix all the ingredients together.
Add a beaten egg to the mixture, then add a few drops of blue food colouring (let the grown-up supervise this and only add it if you want the cakes to be coloured blue – it won't change the flavour if you leave it out).
Mix it all together with your hands and form the dough into small round balls. Place them carefully on to the baking tray and ask the grown-up to put them in the oven for 15 mins.
When the 15 minutes are up, get the grown-up to take the Moonie rock cakes out of the oven, but make sure you leave them to cool before you touch them because they'll be hot! As soon as they've cooled a little, get stuck in! Don't eat too many though, just in case Moonchester and Moonbeam pop round for tea!

ACADEMY GRADUATES
Players To Watch 2008

Jim Cassell gives us the low-down on the seven youngsters who have graduated to a professional contract as of next season.

Curtis Obeng:

"Curtis is a full-back and he's got great pace and is a tough little devil. His feet are getting better all the time and can play left or right-back and he'll benefit from playing and training alongside senior players."

Adam Clayton:

"Adam keeps the ball well, though occasionally wants to be too intricate, and by his own admission knows he has to toughen up a little. He's improved immeasurably over the last 12 months and if he carries on the way he is there is no reason he won't do well over at Carrington, too."

Javan Vidal:

"Jav reminds me of Earl Barrett in many ways – he's a rubber man who bounces all over the place with great athleticism. He's played for England Under-19s this year and, like the rest of the lads, he will benefit immensely from playing alongside senior players."

Gary Breen:

"Gary is a big, craggy centre-half who has played at reserve level. We are working exceptionally hard on his movement, though he has great pace. Like lots of young players, he needs to be more defensively aware and spot danger a little quicker and I think that will be a key for him and Clayton McDonald when they move across to Carrington."

Clayton McDonald:

"Clayton is a central defender, too, and has good feet for a lad who is 6 foot 4 inches tall. He's still filling out physically and has a super attitude and, like Gary Breen, he has plenty of quality. Next year will be a massive one for him."

Paul Marshall:

"Paul is a local lad, a midfielder with a beautiful left-foot – probably the best at the club. He's got great energy and gets around the pitch but needs to improve his running style. He'll get you a goal and can make goals, too, with a first-rate delivery."

Ched Evans:

"We've all got big hopes for Ched because he's a striker and it'll be very interesting to see if he can add the polish needed to play at the highest level. I think Ched was probably our Academy player of the year in 2007."

Gelson Fernandes

SVEN-GORAN ERIKSSON believes new signing Gelson Fernandes is definitely one to watch for the future, though he admits that his chance may come sooner than expected following several impressive displays during pre-season friendlies.

The powerful 20-year-old was Eriksson's second signing as City manager and though little is known in England about Fernandes, his progress was being tracked by several top clubs throughout Europe and the Blues' boss believes he has an outstanding prospect on his hands.

Said Sven: "Gelson is a defensive midfielder and is the captain of the Swiss Under 21 side. He's regarded as one of the biggest talents in Switzerland. He's young, and he looks like he has a great future.

"I'm not sure how much he will play this season, or how much he will start, but it's good for the future if you can find these types of players.

"I'm very pleased with him and while he's been signed with the future in mind, I think he could be one for now as well. He'll be very useful for us this season because he's obviously a good football player."

Fernandes joined the Blues from FC Sion for an undisclosed fee, rumoured to be a Swiss transfer record and has penned a four-year contract. He made 32 starts for the Swiss Super League club last season and has skippered Switzerland's Under 21s on four occasions. He made 99 appearances in all for Sion, scoring one goal in two years.

Cape Verde born Fernandes is excited by the prospect of Premier League football and is still pinching himself that he's now a City player. He said: "I'm still struggling to believe it. I have always worked for a moment like this. I have signed for a famous club. Everything happened so quickly. I am struggling to believe it. My new coach has been successful wherever he has been and I hope to enjoy success with him.

"I want to impose myself at City and then get into the senior national team. I am hungry and motivated. I want to share this happiness with my family and then my friends."

The Boy From Brazil

GEOVANNI Deiderson Mauricio Gomez – Geovanni to his friends – became the first Brazilian to sign for City when he joined the club in the summer. The former Barcelona and Benfica attacking midfielder joined on a free transfer from Brazil side Cruzeiro and said: "It's been a dream for me to play in England, and this is a dream as well to come to a club like Manchester City. It's great to be here after playing in Europe for a few years already.

"Playing in England has been an ambition of mine. I watched a lot of Premier League games when I was at Benfica."

Geovanni arrived at City already in credit having scored a diving header against Manchester United while playing for Benfica during a Champions League clash in 2005. The goal levelled scores and dumped the Reds out of the competition!

"That was a special night for me and for Benfica," he said. "I'm hoping to get more goals like that now that I'm here at City. I think I've got some good experience having played at Barcelona and Benfica, and having played for a few years in Europe I think I'm ready to play in the Premier League."

Born on January 11, 1980 in Acaiaca, Brazil, Geovanni began his career with Cruzeiro as a 17-year-old with immense promise and he was loaned to America aged 18. He was tipped to be one of Brazil's hottest prospects and won four caps, the last of which was in 2003 against Bolivia scoring once for his country.

In 2001 he joined Barcelona for £11m but found it difficult to establish himself in the La Liga giants' midfield, playing just 26 times in two years.

In 2003 he moved to Portuguese giants Benfica, again for £11m and enjoyed a successful three years at the Stadium of Light, playing 91 times and scoring 15 goals. When his contract expired, he opted to return to his first club, Cruzeiro, and he is now hoping to restore his reputation as an exciting attacking midfielder with City - and perhaps force his way back into the Brazil side in the process.

Nedum
Onuoha

Guess Who?

More puzzles to solve - who's hiding on this page?

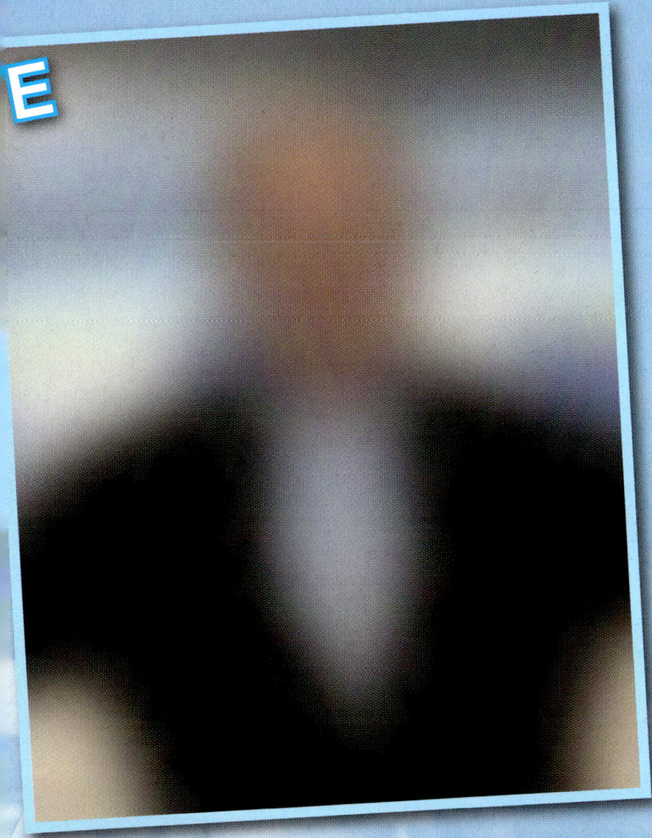

E

F

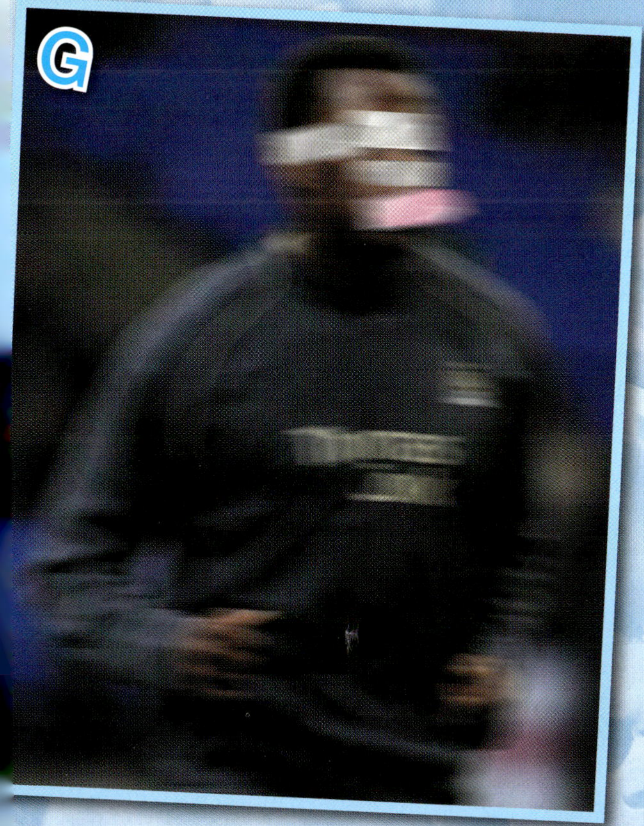

G

H

CitySongsOfPraise

HERE ARE THE SONGS AND CHANTS THAT CITY FANS LOVE TO SING ON A MATCHDAY, HOME OR AWAY. SEE IF YOU KNOW THE TUNES AND PRACTISE THEM SO YOU CAN JOIN IN NEXT TIME YOU'RE AT THE MATCH!

'BLUE MOON'

Blue Moon,
You saw me standing alone,
Without a dream in my heart,
Without a love of my own.

'CITY 'TIL I DIE'

City 'til I die
City 'til I die,
I'm City 'til I die,
I know I am
I'm sure I am
I'm City 'til I die!

'SUPER CITY'

Super City!
We are City,
We are City,
Super City,
from Maine Road,
We are City,
Super City,
We are City from Maine Road!

'HEY MICAH'

Hey Micah you're so fine,
You score your goals in injury time,
Hey Micah!
Hey Micah!

'MY CITY'

You Are My City
My only City,
You make me happy,
When skies are grey,
You'll never know just,
How much I love you,
So please don't take
my City away!

'INVISIBLE MAN'

We are not we're not
really here,
We are not we're not
really here,
Just like the fan of the
Invisible man, we're not
really here

'BOYS IN BLUE'

City - Manchester City,
We are the lads who are
playing to win,
City - the Boys in Blue
will never give in

'SINGING THE BLUES'

I never felt more like
singing the blues,
See City win,
United lose,
Oh City,
You've got me singing
the blues!

	VENUE	SCORE
AUGUST		
20 Chelsea	Stamford Bridge	0 - 3
23 Portsmouth	CoMS	0 - 0
26 Arsenal	CoMS	1 - 0
SEPTEMBER		
11 Reading	Madejski Stadium	0 - 1
17 Blackburn	Ewood Park	2 - 4
20 Chesterfield	The Recreation Ground	1 - 2
23 West Ham	CoMS	2 - 0
30 Everton	Goodison Park	1 - 1
OCTOBER		
14 Sheffield Utd	CoMS	0 - 0
21 Wigan Athletic	JJB Stadium	0 - 4
30 Middlesbrough	CoMS	1 - 0
NOVEMBER		
4 Charlton	The Valley	0 - 1
11 Newcastle	CoMS	0 - 0
18 Fulham	CoMS	3 - 1
25 Liverpool	Anfield	0 - 1
29 Aston Villa	Villa Park	3 - 1
DECEMBER		
4 Watford	CoMS	0 - 0
9 Man Utd	Old Trafford	1 - 3
17 Tottenham	CoMS	1 - 2
23 Bolton	CoMS	0 - 2
26 Sheffield Utd	Bramall Lane	1 - 0
30 West Ham	Upton Park	1 - 0
JANUARY 07		
1 Everton	CoMS	2 - 1
7 Sheffield Wednesday (FA Cup 3)	Hillsborough	1 - 1
13 Bolton	Reebok Stadium	0 - 0
16 Sheffield Wednesday (FA Cup 3 r)	CoMS	2 - 1
20 Blackburn	CoMS	0 - 3
28 Southampton (FA Cup 4)	CoMS	3 - 1
FEBRUARY		
3 Reading	CoMS	0 - 2
10 Portsmouth	Fratton Park	1 - 2
18 Preston (FA Cup 5)	Deepdale	3 - 1
MARCH		
3 Wigan	CoMS	0 - 1
11 Blackburn (FA Cup 6)	Ewood Park	0 - 2
14 Chelsea	CoMS	0 - 1
17 Middlesbrough	Riverside Stadium	2 - 0
31 Newcastle	St James' Park	1 - 0
APRIL		
6 Charlton	CoMS	0 - 0
9 Fulham	Craven Cottage	3 - 1
14 Liverpool	CoMS	0 - 0
17 Arsenal	Emirates Stadium	1 - 3
21 Watford	Vicarage Road	1 - 1
28 Aston Villa	CoMS	0 - 2
MAY		
5 Man Utd	CoMS	0 - 1
13 Tottenham	White Hart Lane	1 - 2

Barclays Premiership – Final table

		P	W	D	L	F	A	GD	pts
1	Manchester United	38	28	5	5	83	27	56	89
2	Chelsea	38	24	11	3	64	24	40	83
3	Liverpool	38	20	8	10	57	27	30	68
4	Arsenal	38	19	11	8	63	35	28	68
5	Tottenham Hotspur	38	17	9	12	57	54	3	60
6	Everton	38	15	13	10	52	36	16	58
7	Bolton Wanderers	38	16	8	14	47	52	- 5	56
8	Reading	38	16	7	15	52	47	5	55
9	Portsmouth	38	14	12	12	45	42	3	54
10	Blackburn Rovers	38	15	7	16	52	54	- 2	52
11	Aston Villa	38	11	17	10	43	41	2	50
12	Middlesbrough	38	12	10	16	44	49	- 5	46
13	Newcastle United	38	11	10	17	38	47	- 9	43
14	Manchester City	38	11	9	18	29	44	- 15	42
15	West Ham United	38	12	5	21	35	59	- 24	41
16	Fulham	38	8	15	15	38	60	- 22	39
17	Wigan Athletic	38	10	8	20	37	59	- 22	38
18	Sheffield United	38	10	8	20	32	55	- 23	38
19	Charlton Athletic	38	8	10	20	34	60	- 26	34
20	Watford	38	5	13	20	29	59	- 30	28

FA Reserve League – Final table

		P	W	D	L	F	A	GD	Pts
1	Bolton Wanderers Reserves	18	10	3	5	21	16	5	33
2	Manchester United Reserves	18	9	4	5	24	17	7	31
3	Middlesbrough Reserves	18	9	3	6	31	25	6	30
4	Manchester City Reserves	18	9	2	7	27	24	3	29
5	Liverpool Reserves	18	8	2	8	24	19	5	26
6	Blackburn Rovers Reserves	18	7	5	6	16	15	1	26
7	Sheffield United Reserves	18	8	2	8	23	23	0	26
8	Newcastle United Reserves	18	6	5	7	29	29	0	23
9	Everton Reserves	18	3	7	8	18	25	- 7	16
10	Wigan Athletic Reserves	18	2	5	11	8	28	- 20	11

Player Stats 2006/07 (all competitions)

No.	Player	Pld	Sub	Gls
1	Andreas Isaksson	12	2	-
25	Joe Hart	1	-	-
2	Micah Richards	34	-	1
3	Michael Ball	14	-	1
16	Nedum Onuoha	16	3	-
17	Jihai Sun	11	3	-
18	Danny Mills	-	1	-
22	Richard Dunne	44	-	1
26	Matthew Mills	1	-	-
5	Ousmane Dabo	14	3	-
7	Stephen Ireland	18	10	3
21	Dietmar Hamann	14	5	-
38	Michael Johnson	10	-	-
43	Ishmael Miller	3	15	-
9	Emile Mpenza	9	2	3
11	Darius Vassell	32	4	5
14	Paul Dickov	9	9	-
20	Georgios Samaras	20	21	6
30	Bernardo Corradi	23	6	3
36	Danny Sturridge	-	2	-

Now left club:

No.	Player	Pld	Sub	Gls
3	Ben Thatcher (now Charlton)	11	-	-
4	Stephen Jordan (released)	15	1	-
8	Joey Barton (now Newcastle)	38	-	7
15	Sylvain Distin (now Portsmth.)	43	-	2
27	Hatem Trabelsi (released)	20	4	1
6	Claudio Reyna (now Red Bull NY)	16	3	-
10	Djamel Abdoun (released)	-	1	-
24	DaMarcus Beasley (loan ended)	13	9	4
28	Trevor Sinclair (released)	16	5	-
12	Nicky Weaver	31	-	-

QuizAnswers

MAZE SOLUTION (From page 39}
FOLLOW THE WHITE PATH

CROSSWORD (From page 25)

Solution:

A B C D E F

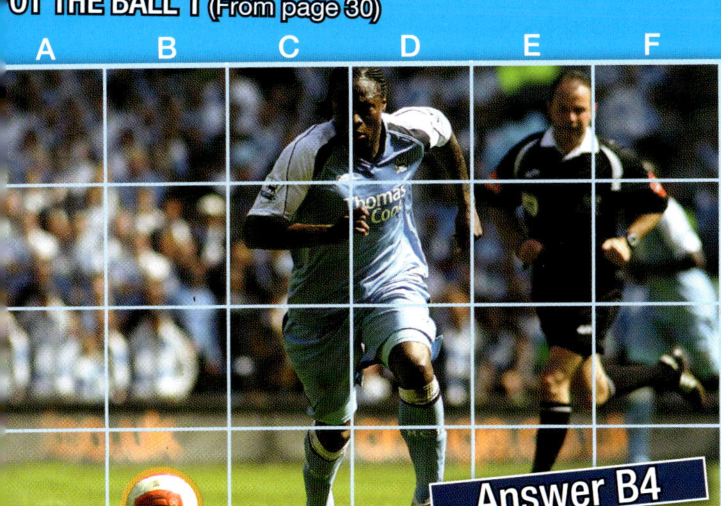

Answer B4

POT THE BALL 2 (From page 30)

A B C D E F

Answer B1/C1

GET THE MESSAGE (From page 42)

Text 1: 'Nedum Onuoha'
Text 2: 'Sweden' & 'Andreas Isaksson'
Text 3: 'Richard Dunne'
Text 4: 'Micah Richards'

TALK A GOOD GAME (From page 35)

THE MISSING PLAYERS' NAMES ARE – IN ORDER:

1 Ishmael Miller & Georgios Samaras

2 Darius Vassell & Bernardo Corradi

3 Bernardo Corradi & Micah Richards

4 Michael Ball & Darius Vassell

5 Hatem Trabelsi, Bernardo Corradi & Michael Ball

SPOT THE DIFFERENCE (From page 43)

Richard Dunne's shirt badge is missing (chest)
Richard Dunne's Premiership badge is missing (arm)
Ryan Giggs' shirt badge is missing (chest)
Michael Carrick's shirt badge is missing (chest)
Roof is missing (top left corner)
'Mcfc.co.uk' is missing from Level 2 advertising boards
'MCFC' is missing off Dunne's sock (left leg)
Sylvain Distin's shirt badge is missing (chest)
City crest is missing off Level 2 advertising board
'Thomas Cook' is missing off Michael Ball's shirt